The Complete Food Service Operation Handbook

by Joshua Embry

The purpose of this Operational Handbook is to enable your operation to thrive. It tackles everything from how to plan and price menus, how to train your staff to sell, HACCP Food Safety and Requirements, and How to safely use most if not all of the commercial equipment in your kitchen. Beyond this it explores how to manage customer service in relation to customer perception as well as an understanding of metrics and how they can function within your operation.

This volume contains:

Pricing Menus
(Really Understanding Your Pricing Needs)

Menu Planning
(A Guide For Cafés, Coffee Shops, and Quick Serve Food Service)

Pocket Sales Training Guide
(Create a Sales Culture in 5 minutes)

General HACCP and Food Safety Training
(Condensed Safety Training/Refresher/HACCP)

Complete Kitchen Safety Training with Safety Sign-off Sheets for:
(Griddle/Flat Tops/Tilts, Convection/Non-Convection Ovens, Dish machines, Free Standing and Counter-Top Mixers, Refrigerator/Freezer Training, Meat Slicer Safety, and Stove-tops)

Battling Perception
(The reality behind customer service and the dreaded survey)

The Metric Game

Pricing Menus

Really Understanding Your Pricing Needs
By Joshua R. Embry

Introduction

Whether you've been there from day one or inherited someone else's operation, you need to cost your menu correctly to keep your doors open. This can be a difficult task if you make it that way or it can be a simple as taking a little bit of time out of one afternoon. Why not get it done today?

The misconception of pricing menus is that you've got to tackle everything at once, this simply isn't true. Quite frankly, I'd say its preferred to narrow your focus.

Why narrow your focus? There's the time factor, what do you really have time to do? Then there's the sticker-shock factor. You want to update or create menu pricing that works for your business needs, but especially if you've been around for a while, you want to avoid running off your patrons with massive changes. Avoid this if you can. It's very different if you're opening your shop or restaurant for the first time. If it's the first go at a menu, then you can still use the tips below, but don't make the mistake of hastily throwing something together.

Where to start?

What are your top performers if you're an existing establishment? List out the top 5. Not from your gut feelings, but from your actual sales data. These are what we'll work with in phase 1. If you're a new establishment, do some research, use Google or ask similar establishment managers around you what their key top selling items are. You don't have the advantage of knowing what actually sells in your location yet, so you're stuck making an educated guess. Keep in mind that we're not talking about just throwing numbers out there. Read a few articles, talk to people to figure out what your best sellers will likely be. In most cases it's beverages, in others a burger, others fries, etc.

Once you figure out what your top 5 actual or projected sellers are, do a cost analysis.
Let's say you're looking at Fries (substitute your actual item here.)
Where do you buy it from? How much does it cost per ounce?

Here's your example: *Keep in mind that I'm not teaching you how to sell fries, this can be any product.*

Crinkle Cut Fries: 30 lbs case, price: $21.50
I break it down to per lb cost. $21.50/30lbs = $0.716666 , let's round up to $0.72 per lb.
There are 16 oz in a lb, so take the $0.72 and divide it by 16 ounces. We get $.045.

So every ounce of fries costs you four and a half cents. This doesn't include your overhead costs such as building lease, electricity, gas for the fryer, wages, insurance, or employee benefits, etc. For now let's keep it simple.

Now you decide what your portion size is going to be. Are you going to serve 8 oz of fries or 10?

If you serve 8 oz of fries, take $.045 X 8 ounces = $0.36 per 8 oz serving.
This still isn't your true cost. What are you serving fries in? A dish? A paper tray?
Cost out your expense. It's realistic that either your dishwashing chemicals or paper tray are going to cost you about $0.04 per serving per item. Use this generic cost if you are unsure.

$0.36 fries + $.04 container = $0.40 total cost, less overhead.
Now it's difficult to calculate your overhead on a per item basis, it's usually easier to factor this into a total gross margin calculation on total sales needed to cover monthly costs, we'll deal with this later on.

If you want every menu item to roughly cover some of the estimated overhead costs you can add 35% to your menu item cost. This will give you a rough basis that can be looked at later on when fine tuning your menu.

Assuming your cost of $0.40 per fry serving, let's add on 35%. ($0.40 X 1.35) That gives us a true cost of $0.54 each serving. Now you know where to begin with pricing.
You'll want to double your investment if possible on all sides and beverages.

So you wouldn't want your bottom line price to be less than $1.08 per serving. Keep in mind that you aren't trying to give things away for free either. Your goal is to turn a profit. The balance is going to be finding a price that will lead to more sales and increase your total profit margins.

Check around and see what other restaurants or stores are charging for similar products. They may be way off base with incorrectly priced menus, so just use them as a reference point, don't just copy their prices. For all you know, they could be going out of business!

For fries, now, in 2015 I would charge around $2.00 for 8 oz. That provides a nice profit margin but isn't so high that you're going to turn people's heads. You're giving them half a pound of fries, that's a lot. You now have the option to play around with size and price. Do you want to offer one size of fries or a variety? Small could be 6 ounces, Medium 8 ounces, and Large could be 10 ounces if you wanted. It's your menu, do what you want with it. If you're pricing is high, look at lowering the portion size that you give them.

For your calculations I recommend either converting things to ounces or eaches. For example if you're selling corn on the cob, count 1 cob as an each. If you're selling rice, price it by dry ounce. (When you cook rice you increase it's weight by adding water).

Let's review what we've just done with fries, and make a template for your other items.

1) What do I pay for a case or minimum quantity of this item? _____
2) What is the smallest reasonable portion I can break this down to? _____
   (Steaks could be 1 each, rice could be in ounces, etc.) What's the cost per unit:_____
3) How many portions do I want to serve per order? (how many ounces, eaches, etc.)_____
4) What's the cost to deliver to the customer? (paper plate, plastic forks, soap, etc.)_____
5) Add 35% for overhead costs:_____
6) Double this above cost to produce a profit: _____
7) Research similar item pricing online or from competitors, what is the average price:_____
8) Do I need to raise or lower the price to be competitive? New price: _____

Keep in mind that price alone isn't the determining factor on consumer purchasing. The bottom line is that they need to see value in your item or service.

A perfect example was when I priced a 32 ounce fountain soda at $2.50. In theory I would have had a great profit margin and it was in line with competition. In actuality I only sold a handful, so while each sale generated a decent individual profit, the total combined sales were low. Where we differed from competition was location. I have seasonal visitors so that factored in. Once I lowered the margin on the soda and reduced the total price, I began to sell more and realize more overall profits. So while the soda was now $1.50, and I only made $1.00 profit per sale, I had 10 times as many sales, so it more than made up for the pricing change. This will be the most challenging and fun aspect of your menu, pricing to draw in sales while increasing overall profits.

Remember that your pricing isn't set in stone, usually... So either make the appropriate pricing changes as needed, or close your doors! I recommend reevaluating every year, unless some drastic market fluctuation has occurred. Did your beef cost go up 20%? Then it's time to reevaluate beef items RIGHT NOW. Don't throw your money away all year until you look at it again.

Repeat this process for your top 5 sellers or projected sellers. This book doesn't go into menu development and product placement or the psychology behind purchasing decisions, but I will give you some basic tips here.

Don't over clutter your menu. (it distracts customers from purchasing)
Do group things logically. (If I want a coffee, they should all be on the same part of the menu)
Do use uniformity. (Use similar colors, make pricing all one color, etc. so it's easy to navigate)

Here's the most effective pricing example I've used:

Item:	Single Serving	Combo
Chicken Nuggets (8 pc)	$3.50	$5.50

Looking at this pattern, you've found a consistent way to upsell your combo offering. If you don't offer a combo, you may want to consider it. The guest's eyes will scroll to the combo pricing first, then correct and find the single serving price. What you've successfully done with this setup is got the customer to already consider the combo versus the single serving. This will boost your sales and create customer's upselling themselves. It will also make it easier for your cashier or waitstaff to upsell since the guest has already seen the combo option.
I've put the example in a table above to keep it easy, you don't have to set it up that way. We don't have lines or the label "Item" at our location. This small change has really driven up sales and profits at our location.

Conclusion

Once you've made appropriate menu pricing changes on your top selling items, see how things go. Give it a few weeks, have your profits increased? Have your top selling items changed? Reevaluate until you get the results you want.

A tip, if you haven't priced out your beverages, do it now. You can't always add a food item on, but you'll likely have guests that want to order a drink of some kind. Drinks will always have a higher attachment rate with a food item than anything else, so please make them a priority, they could literally be the thing that keeps you afloat and your doors open.

Now that you've made some changes and have the basic principle of pricing menus down, play with your numbers. See what your true overhead costs are, write them out. How many days are you open per month? Divide your total overhead cost by the number of days you're open each month. This is your daily minimum sales goal to keep the lights on. Then add in your cost of food etc. Do you need to increase your prices to help meet these needs? In our example we used an estimated 35% increase to help cover overhead costs, do you need to increase that to 50%? Do it. Adjust the formula to meet your actual needs.

Fine tune what you can. Do you notice you primarily sell fried items from 11am-7pm, look at turning the fryer off, or only up half way during hours outside of that time. Do you notice employees leaving lights on? Install a few motion sensor switches to lower your overall electrical costs. Look for waste and eliminate it wherever you can. Are you always throwing out salad? Order less. Do you have a menu item that rarely is sold? Consider getting rid of it, or increasing the price. If you increase the price it can make keeping it around more worthwhile. Keep your higher labor foods priced higher than your quick-serve items. For example, it takes roughly 3 minutes to cook an order of fries, and it can take up to 8 minutes for a fresh made burger. Price your quick serve items lower than those longer cooking items. This will help drive your sales to the quick-serve high profit items and you'll save on labor. Continue to look at your best-selling items and adjust the pricing when it makes sense. These are the items you are really selling, continue to price them up until you see sales going down or flat lining, then bring them back down a bit if you're still able. Find that sweet spot where you still have a strong demand for the item but can maximize your profits.

Lastly, menu placement. You'll want your high profit, high selling items listed prominently on your menu boards, with top listing, or on your menus. You can even highlight them in a special section (ultimately listing them twice) in a menu or on table card advertisements.

You've got the tools, now use them to sell like you never have before. You can do this!

For selling tips, see my other books on Amazon.

Menu Planning: A Guide For Cafés, Coffee Shops, and Quick Serve Food Service

(Quick Pocket Guide Edition)

By Joshua R. Embry

Whether your menus are posted above your registers, on printed handouts, or even online, your guests have specific patterns they use to pick out what they want.

They either already know what they want and are just trying to find it on your menu or they have no idea what they're after. Either way, your menu placement needs to be planned out in a way that is easy to read, is consistent in appearance, and really brings focus to your high profit items.

Let's face it, if you give premium menu space to your low-profit items you won't be in business for very long.

There are a few tips and tricks to making sure your menu catches the eyes of your guest.

The first key element is to pick a consistent color scheme. Once you select your colors, stick with them. Are you labeling the item in blue and the price in white? Whatever it is, make it consistent across the board to avoid confusing your customers.

Next, you'll want to organize your menu into logical sections. Some examples would be:

Drinks, Foods, and Snacks

These are main categories, if you have many items you may want to break them down even further: from drinks to hot drinks/cold drinks, and Foods to Fried Foods/Grilled Foods, and Snacks to Hot or Cold (ice cream versus nachos, etc.)

Once you have a basic structure (see the example below):

Beverages	Food	Ice Cream

Once you've decided on a layout, it's time to add items.

Let's say you sell fountain drinks, specialty coffee, and shakes or ice cream. It's time to look at your highest profit items. Don't guess, sit down and figure out what things cost, and compare them to what you sell them for. What are your highest profit items? You likely want to focus on high profit dollars instead of %. Ultimately it's the total dollars you make that will keep you in business. See my other book titled: Pricing Menus to find out more about how to correctly price your items. Assuming you've already got a handle on this, we'll move forward with product placement on your menu.

The top left areas of your menus are prime areas, but so are the bottoms. So be sure to use these areas to your advantage.

One example was for our establishment; we had determined our best bet for profit with hot food was our combo options, so we utilized the top left area of the menu to list our top 3 profit items. Then we priced add-ons in columns. If you'd like to learn more about the benefits of add-ons and selling techniques, check out my other book, _Pocket Sales Training Guide: Create a Sales Culture in 5 minutes_. The bottom line is that add-on sales increase your overall profit if done right.

In our combo menu, we listed the burger in the first column, then as a combo to the right, so they could see the value in creating a combo meal. It looked something like this:

Grill			Coffee	Ice Cream/Milkshakes
	Single	Combo		Single Scoop $1.50
Hartland Burger	$5.00	$8.00	Regular: $2.00	Addtl scoops $1.00 ea.
Spicy Chicken Sndw	$4.00	$6.00		
Chicken Nuggets	$3.50	$5.00	Specialty Coffee: $4.00	Milkshakes: $4.75
Mozzarella Sticks	$3.50	$5.00	Cappuccino, Frapp,	
		w/ soda	Espresso, ….	Chocolate, Vanilla, Strawberry,
Beer Battered Fries	$3.50	$4.50		Cookie Dough, Mint Chip
Crinkle Cut Fries	$2.50	$3.50	Add-on Syrups: $.50/ea	
Fountain Soda: Sm. $1.50 Lrg. $2.00				

Keep in mind our menu was handwritten and contained a few more items than this, but this an example of what you'd want to do.

There is no guesswork as to what things cost, and pricing is clear. You can see we used a column-method to increase our add-on sales. So for a single burger you'd pay $5 or to make it a combo it would be $8.00. Once we got out of the combo selections we moved into a soda being the add-on and so you see the "w/ soda" addition, meaning "with soda". The customer already sees how much it is with a soda and so when you pitch the add-on at the register they're more likely to accept it.

Also notice how the fountain sodas were placed at the bottom. They area high profit item and they were purposefully placed here. A small soda cost roughly $.25 and a large about $.50 more or less. So these items represent a high dollar profit compared to the cost to sell. Notice as well how the Coffee area is displayed. Instead of multiple prices for varying drinks, a standard price was developed for any of our deemed specialty coffees. This reduces clutter as well as frees up space compared to writing the price for every single drink.

An additional technique for making an item on your menu pop is white space. Notice how the milkshakes are off by themselves. This makes them contrast the background better and stand out. Shakes cost around $1.25 to produce and selling them for $4.75 creates a large revenue stream for our café. On the other side of the coin, making them takes time and we can easily do over 100 per day. Shakes cover my wages for 3-4 workers alone, so are vital for our success.

The last tip is that it is okay to have off menu items. These should be your convenience options that are not your high profit items. An example would be adding your burger sauce to fries, something where you're not really going to make a profit and in our case we wouldn't want to waste the resource (burger sauce) to smother someone's fries since our sauce costs a bit to make. In reality we would probably break even if it became popular to sell as an add-on. The downfall would be the added labor of making more sauce in the middle of a busy shift, slowing down service and decreasing customer satisfaction. But, you will have a customer who asks, so it's best to take care of their needs and at least break even in the process.

If you're also going to have printed menus, keep the font the same. Section titles should have a larger font size than the menu items. Group items as they make sense (salads with salads, etc.). Your main item should be in bold and your description should not be. Italics can also be used to share extra information. View the example on the next page.

Entrées:

Carne Asada Tacos $6.99

Your choice of beef, pork, or grilled chicken.

Enchilada Sampler $8.99

Comes with 1 chicken, 1 beef, 1 pork, and 1 cheese enchilada smothered in red or green sauce.

Taquito Special $6.99

8 Beef taquitos served with shredded lettuce and fresh guacamole.

Grande Nachos $5.99

Your choice of beef, or grilled chicken on top of our fresh tortilla chips with melted cheese

El Gordo Burrito $11.99

Beef or shredded pork 2lb burrito filled with cheese, rice, and black beans.

Menu structure and planning really is this simple. This is a short pocket guide edition to help you get the vital information that you need on your menus without investing hours reading hundreds of pages backing up claims or listing research and studies as to why you should do this or that. This guide is simple, straightforward, and to the point. Often, that's all a real business owner has time for.

Pocket Sales Training Guide

Create a Sales Culture in 5 minutes

Whether you're leading sales in a retail big box environment or in a quick-serve restaurant, there are key tips to driving sales through trainable behaviors. If you don't take time to invest in your staff you won't see sales growth, it's as simple as that.

Book Sections:

Time Investment

Credentials

The Heart of the Matter

People Make the Difference

Case Study

Limited Options

Full Time versus Part Time

Shift Preference

Set Clear Expectations

One-on-One training

New Hires

Training 1: Average Ticket

Training 2: Consumer Confidence

Training 3: Asking the Right Questions

Training 4: Gross Margin

Cashiers

Closing

Time Investment:

If you're serious about creating a sales culture in your establishment you've got to be serious about investing in your employees. This doesn't mean taking hours every week to drill the same boring information down your employees throats, but it does mean *purposefully engaging your staff with the goal of change*. I try to focus on short 5 minute themes that you can share with your teams at the start of a shift. If you aren't starting your shift with a quick 1-2 minute team briefing, you're hurting your process.

Credentials:

The first thing we should discuss is why you want to listen to these guidelines in the first place.

Here's a little about my background, this isn't a pat on the back, rather showing that I'm brining useful tools from the real world.

OfficeMax Inc.: Sales Specialist, Technical Liaison, ASM Sales Manager

Amerisource Bergen Pharmaceuticals Operations Manager - Distribution Center Management

Sprint Nextel: Retention Specialist, Quality Analyst within the Data and Analytics Department, Advanced Technical Support

Hume Lake Christian Camps - Food Service Coordinator

Hartland Christian Camp - Food Service Director

The Heart of the Matter

You've likely heard it before, but customers are key to your sales. Over the years there have been psychological studies into the behaviors of consumers and many big box retailers subscribe to the fundamental principles of these studies. Through each organization I've worked with I have learned basic strategies for bringing up profits and reducing overhead costs. We'll explore these below.

People Make the Difference.

This is a basic concept that really rings true. I've made the mistake of keeping people on the sales team who simply couldn't sell early on in my career and my establishment and I suffered for it. Don't make this mistake. <u>Ultimately YOU are responsible for your sales culture and nice people that don't know how to sell won't get it done for you</u>. They may be nice people, they may have great qualities in other areas like attendance, but the fundamental issue is that unless you have the right person, you will never see the results you need.

Now, there are two main reasons that I've found that people are not the sales individuals that you need. The first is that they are not willing to be that person. The second is that they do not have the proper skills to be that person.

These are two serious differences. An employee not willing to try your strategies or follow your trainings or engage your customer is one that is apathetic. They will not be motivated and you must usher them out the door as soon as you can. Hire their replacement today.

An employee that does not have the skill to do the job has hope. The great thing about an employee without any skills is that you can train them specifically to your sales environment. Each time they learn something new and use it they become more and more valuable to your overall operation. They must be willing to learn, and often they are the most eager to learn because they know that they do not have a skill. These are my favorite employees. With some investment they will become your best performers and will remain loyal to your organization.

Case Study

This is a real life example. I had an employee that complained about his wages asking me if I expected him to take the job seriously at such low pay. By the way, at the time, the pay was $1/hr above minimum wage and he was only a 12-15 hour per week college student. I spoke with him for a few minutes and end the end made the following deal. I would give him a $.25/hr raise and he would improve his selling skills to appropriate levels within 30 days. He balked at the rate increase and I stated this was the first stage, if he really improved his performance not only would he be eligible for more hours but that I would be willing to look at his pay after another 90 days of performance. Against my better judgment I gave the small pay increase with expected results. His attitude didn't change, he didn't work any harder, but one thing did happen. After 30 days, he never complained about his pay again because he understood it was based on his efforts and he knew he wasn't meeting expectations. He left shortly thereafter.

The lesson: extra money didn't improve his performance. His basic issue was apathy and he was never going to become the sales person that I needed him to be. He naturally progressed out of position on his own, but at what cost? What would my quarterly results have been like had I hired a new employee sooner?

Limited Options

Let's face it, not everyone has a spiff or commission sales program, even those that do don't always make sense. Somehow at a big box retailer I was supposed to motivate my sales staff to sell key items like insurance for a spiff of a few pennies. Bottom line, I did not motivate my staff successfully this way and every moment I tried was a wasted opportunity for real and useful training for my staff. Follow your company guidelines and training, it's part of your job to be on board with corporate. Don't simply think this will work. You've got to go beyond this if you want real change.

So great, we spoke about what options we don't have. What about options we do have. Here are some creative ways to use the tools that you do have to manage your sales team.

First, total hours. You may be limited here, but you may not. At one location we had a cap of 24 hrs/week for part timers and a minimum of 9 hours to stay employed. I successfully used these guidelines to foster a sales environment. When I hired a new part time staff member I let them know I was going to work them about 12-15 hrs a week on average with more or less based on performance. I also let them know that they had a few weeks to get acclimated where they would be trained and given an opportunity to learn the skills needed to succeed before their hours were updated. This was a great tool.

Many sales managers are graded on key metrics such as total sales dollars, gross margin, add-ons, targeted promotions, and loyalty programs. If you're not your own boss, find out what you're being measured against. Hitting your numbers is key to remaining employed. You have to find out what numbers are the most important to your organization. Ours was focused on average ticket, gross margin, insurance, and loyalty subscriptions. For those not familiar I'll quickly cover what these key metrics are. Average ticket is simply the total amount of money the average customer spends. So say 10 customers represented $250 in sales that hour. So your average ticket was $250/10 = $25 per customer. This is a great average ticket. Many locations chase an average ticket of around $10 per customer. Gross Margin simply represents your profit after cost. So let's say you sell a $100 printer. That printer cost your store $95, and you sold it for $100 without any coupons or discounts. This means you made a gross margin of $5 ($100-$95=$5). This number is often represented as a percentage in a sales report. So $5 is 5% of the $100, meaning your gross margin for that sale was 5%.

Full Time versus Part Time

Another tool you have is controlling your employee types. Your Full Time Employee positions are limited, likely you're forced to work with mostly part time individuals. You can reward part timers who excel by promoting them to Full Time when a position opens. Not everyone has this option. If you don't, then continue to reward your high performers with more hours, even if they just get 2-4 more hours per week, it does help. The more time your key employees are present, the more quality sales you'll get.

Shift Preference:

Let's face it, you should know when your sales are taking place. If you don't know the busiest times of your sales day, look it up now, or ask your data team to figure it out. Many POS systems have an hourly report option, look at it over a 12 month period. This tells you on average when your busiest times are. Reports are your friends, don't be afraid of them, learn how to read them. Once you know your key sales times, plan your sales force around them. You want your key individuals present when the majority of your sales occur. You'll see an increase in sales and margin when you have real sellers in the environment. It would be a waste to have a key sales person working during your down times. Find out what shifts employees like, and based on their performance work to more closely alight their schedule to those times whenever possible. A happy performer is going to perform even more for you.

Set Clear Expectations:

Not everyone is going to perform exactly the same way, it's just a simple fact, and no amount of training can really manipulate that. You can take a nonperformer and turn them into a performer but there are those that have more natural abilities than others. Reward progress. If your employee sold 1 insurance item the week before and this week they sold two, it's a big deal! That's a 100% increase in a week. Don't undervalue that improvement even though another employee gets 3-4 per week. They might get there as well, but it will take some time. Let your team know their daily, weekly, and monthly goals. This is why I can't stress the importance of a 1-3 minute start of the day sales huddle. You can call them out by name. "Joe, you need to get 2 insurance add-ons today, alright? I'm here to help, let's do this", "Sally, you're doing great on insurance, keep it up, but I'd really like to see you selling more paper with printers." etc. Let your team know the daily goal, is it 10 insurance add-ons for the day? Let them know, and push them to get there. Let them know your sales goal for the day, is it $14,000? Do you have 7 sales members that day? If they're all working the same total hours they should all work to personally sell $2,000 that day. Goals can be calculated with limited effort, know them well.

One-on-One training:

<u>If you don't train individuals you won't get individual results</u>. Often I see team trainings where the thought is the shotgun mentality. If you simply throw it at the whole team maybe some of them will remember or use it. While some trainings could benefit from a team environment, I haven't found that skill-specific training works well in this arena. Here's an example. You're telling your crew that you now sell a new type of camera. This would be a great team meeting or training. If you want your average ticket to go up, you'd invest your time more wisely if you trained one-on-one.

But you're busy, you don't have time for one-on-one training. I cannot stress this enough, you need to invest in training! BUT, here's the catch - you only have to train one person. I've found that part of reinforcing training is requiring your staff to teach each other. I've used this in sales and in food service. Take the time to train one employee- your best employee something. For average sales you could walk the store with your employee and talk about add-ons, or recommending higher dollar products. These are two simple ways to build your average ticket. Ask them questions, make them answer, make them role play briefly. In regards to role-playing, don't make it awkward. A team environment is very awkward and often they are more nervous in a group setting than they would be in a customer setting. Look at a printer with your employee and ask them what they could sell with it. A printer cable? Extra ink? Insurance? Next, tell them not to overwhelm a customer. Don't offer 5 add-ons. Pick one or two and leave it at that. Go over gross margin with them. Which of those add-ons produce the greatest profit for your store? The printer cable? That's what they should pitch. This is an example, you'll come up with your own ideas together, it's not that hard, just do it. So now you've invested 5-15 minutes on one employee. When your customer-base is slower have that employee take another employee through the same training you gave them. They'll put it in their own words, but you've effectively utilized other staff to train for you and you've reinforced that training in the original employee. Now both the first and second employee can train others. Ideally you'd want your best performers to do the training first and you'd want those performers to provide the training to others. Having a low performer train others is not what you want happening.

Later on you'll move to your next training, and you may need to spend 5-15 minutes with an employee now and again, you should plan to do this at least once a week. But that's it. You could, in theory, train your entire sales team with a 5 minute per week investment of your time. The more you do this, the faster the training will become. Your staff will gain an understanding of what the training is about and run with it. If your staff isn't running with it, it's time to hire new staff.

New Hires

New hires are your bread and butter. It's likely you came into position through a vacancy. Hopefully the person before you retired or got promoted, but let's face it, often in sales they didn't meet the criteria and were moved on. You may have inherited someone else's bad decisions but you don't have to live with them. I've seen defeated managers say they had no other options, you do have options, use them. I've already gone over how you can utilize hours to your advantage. If you have a team of 9 people, shaving 1 hour off of each means you now have 9 hours per week to hire a part time staff member. Obviously you don't want to rob from your top performers but this is just a simplified example. This will do two things. First, it will let your staff know you're serious. You haven't threatened anyone, that doesn't work, but you have let them know that they are getting less hours and you're looking to hire someone new. Sometimes this step alone changes the sales environment and you may end up not hiring anyone new because people finally understand and perform. Chances are you'll have one or two stragglers that don't get it and you'll dwindle their hours down or let them go to make room for a better sales staffer.

New hires represents fresh canvas for you to paint your views on. You can set clear expectations early on. Let them know that sales rules and hours will be given first to performers after their training time is complete. Drill into their minds early on that you have expectations that need to be met. It's easier to refer to this later on if they aren't performing. Communicate your needs to them. "I need someone who can increase each sale for every customer and offer our insurance." "Can you do that?" Then you're off to the right start. Don't rush the hiring process. Interview 1-3 individuals as soon as possible. If you don't see potential, don't hire them. Nothing prevents stacking a great sales team more than filling up your spots because you rushed the process. I understand you have needs, you have shifts to fill, you NEED that cashier yesterday. This book isn't about reacting to your day-to-day needs, it's about changing or creating a sales environment in your establishment. That's the only thing that will change your results. Over time you will have a sales team that you recruited, likely a blend of already existing staff with new behaviors and new hires that you've trained from the ground up.

Now that we've covered some basic managerial aspects of the sales culture, it's time to get into the quick trainings. Remember these work best on an individual basis. The quick 5 minute trainings are based on sales themes such as average ticket and will help your team meet those metrics.

Training 1: Average Ticket

Intro:

You cannot impact every customer purchase that comes through your door, but you can impact most.

The goal of today's training is to help you add value and dollars to your customer's purchase. In order to successfully increase a customer's order you have to provide value. That value can be as simple as an ice cold water bottle that you're selling up near the register. There are two things at play here, *benefit statements* and *consumer confidence*.

A customer will not purchase an item without a perceived value- you need a benefit statement.

Let's focus on that bottled water. It's hot outside, here's your statement.

"Wow it sure is hot outside, would you like to me to grab you one of these ice cold water bottles for the road? It's only $1." (etc.)

Your benefit statement includes the fact that the ice cold water will help against the heat outside. You also helped increase their consumer confidence by using the word "only" in your price presentation. In their mind they are processing what you said "it's only $1". Many customers will accept this offer. They know they should drink more water, it sure is hot outside and before you mentioned it they never would have thought of it. You just increased your average ticket.

Another example, a printer:

"That sure is a great printer, how about you get these replacement cartridges today as well so you know you'll have ink when you need it." Put the ink in their hands. Customer's want to avoid conflict or discomfort and will usually appreciate the suggestion that will add less hassle to them later on. Ink is a high profit item, if you can add that to the printer sale you've not only increased your average ticket, you've increased your gross margin. Great, what if they say no because there's ink in the box.

"That's true but often you'll find starter cartridges in new printers that aren't full capacity, so you might run out after 10-15 pages, I was just trying to help avoid that frustration."

This is actually a true statement, I've seen it happen, to the point a customer wanted to return the printer because they thought that was the ink capacity. I let them know the starter scenario and they asked why no one told them that before. So you've solved the average ticket goal and improved customer satisfaction. If they say no, at least you know they'll need paper to print on. Engage the customer, ask them what they are looking to print - photos, just documents, etc. You can use this info to upgrade to glossy paper for photos or grab them a case of paper if it's going to be for a big project at work.

Your turn (employee)

What do you sell the most of? What are 1-3 add-ons that make sense for that item.

Now, go sell them.

Training 2: Consumer Confidence

There are a great number of well informed customers using smart phones and ingenuity to make purchasing decisions. But just because they've read it doesn't mean they are 100% confident with their decision. You need to boost their confidence. First, make sure what they are getting is right for their needs. Ask questions that will give you more information. Sometimes a customer is caught between more than one product and will decide not to purchase any due to the difficulty in the decision. This is where you can recommend a product. Why do you recommend it? Is it a good brand? Are other customers happy with their purchase?

"I definitely understand wanting to pick the right one. I know that most of my customers go with product x and seem to be pretty happy with it."

"Well, "product x" can print 5 pages a minute, "product y "can print 12, if it were me, I'd go with "product y", I don't think you can go wrong with "product y".

Another tactic you could use to boost consumer confidence is assuming the sale. Once you've provided a benefit statement and some consumer confidence statements, start finalizing the sale, assume they're on board and move onto the next step. If it's a restaurant move forward. Let's say they were deciding on nuggets versus fries, you recommended nuggets because fries are all carbs and nuggets are high in protein (great benefit statement by the way).

So you'd say *"Okay, so did you want to get an ice cold soda with your nuggets?"*

You've assumed they have agreed with you and are now moving to your add-on.

Don't worry, they'll let you know if they haven't decided yet. Now there's an opportunity to continue to get their buy-in. One great tactic is mentioning the return period when nothing else is working.

"You know, we've got a great return policy, why don't you take it home, try it out for a few days, keep the receipt and if by this time next week it's not meeting your needs, just bring it back, find me and I'll help you exchange it for something else, sound good?"

I hate to say it, but even if it didn't meet their needs, some won't return it. But you know what, if you've really listened to their needs and recommended a product that should meet those needs, you've done your part. If you hadn't helped them they wouldn't have gotten anything and their needs really wouldn't have been met then.

Keeping your customers happy is a key in regards to repeat business and sales, but if you've sincerely made your best recommendation based on their communicated needs, don't feel bad. They could have left something out. This training is on consumer confidence.

Training 3: Asking the Right Questions

You need to ask questions and listen to your customers. The first question should be permission to assist them. *"Hi, I'm Josh, is there anything I can help you with today?"* If they don't want your help, don't linger. Stay in the area in case they need help, but move on to another customer.

If they do want your help, listen to what they say, reword the question and ask it back to them if you don't fully understand.

Customer: *"I need a thing for my phone so I can hear"*

Sales Person: *" Okay, do you mean a blue-tooth headset for your cell phone?"*

Customer: *"No, I need something for my office desk phone"*

Sales Person: *"Oh okay, let's head over to that area of the store and find what you need."*

Asking the right question can save you and the customer a lot of time.

Customer: "I'm looking for a printer."

Sales Person: "Okay, I can definitely help you with that, what are you wanting to do with your printer, print photos or mostly just documents?"

Customer: "Oh I hadn't thought of photos, that might be nice. I'll mostly be printing documents but photos would be nice as well."

Sales Person: "Alright, let's find you a printer that can do both and go over some options."

Server: "Welcome to Bob's Cafe, what can I get started for you today?"

Guest: "Well, I haven't really decided yet."

Server: "Did you want some more time to look over the menu or some help in deciding?"

Scenario 1

Guest: "Just some more time is fine"

Server: "No problem, I'll be back over in a bit, take your time"

Scenario 2

Guest: "Well, I'm trying to decide on the burger or chicken sandwich"

Server: "Do you like spicy food?"

Guest: "Not really, why?"

Server: "That's our spicy chicken sandwich"

Guest: "Oh my, okay then ,let's go with the burger."

While not all of these scenarios will match your needs, you should be able to get the picture. Don't ask yes or no questions, get to the heart of what they need as quickly as you can.

Training 4: Gross Margin

Gross margin won't translate over to your customer, but it's the most important part of your sales business. If you sell $1,000,000 in product and make no profit, you're out of business. That's it, game over. If you sell $10,000 in product and make $9,000 profit, you're doing the right thing. Now these are exaggerated scenarios but you get the picture, you're here to make money.

Your staff needs to know what makes your business money, what keeps the lights on?

In most electronics stores, it's ink. Ink in some sales locations can easily represent a 60% profit per sale. So any easy training for your employee is to have the observe where customers are in the store and reach out to them even more if they are in a high gross margin area. In my store, if a customer was at the ink wall, so was a sales person. If they were in furniture the same applied as at my store furniture typically had a 40% profit margin.

If it's a restaurant, your quick serve high gross margin items are typically drinks and fried foods. They require very little labor and produce a nice return on profits. Train your servers to recommend fries or add-on drinks to orders.

Find out what your high profit items are, don't assume, run a report or reach out to someone who can. A nifty trick is to visibly mark a pricing label with a pen mark or dot. Teach your sales staff that dotted items have a high gross margin and if possible should be something considered when making a recommendation. By training them to simply look for the mark, you can improve your gross margin.

Cashiers are the last chance for a gross margin and average ticket boost. Why do we care about average ticket? For the most part increased sales can also mean increased gross margin. If someone buys a notepad for $2 and you add on a pack of pens for $1, you boosted your average ticket to $3. If the notepad had a $1 gross margin profit, and the pens had a $.50 gross margin profit, now you took what would have been $1 of profit and turned it into $1.50. Not much, but that's a 50% increase in your gross margin for that sale, THAT IS A BIG DEAL. Now take that across the board and you're seeing nothing like you've ever seen before. Your boss's boss is going to take notice and visit your store and ask what you're doing differently. Trust me, that's what happened to me. I had a national executive request to specifically visit my store while they were in our state because of our results in a category.

Know your high gross margin items, make them easily recognized by your staff, and train them to recommend and sell them and you will see increased profits, and likely a bonus if your pay is based on performance metrics.

Cashiers

Cashiers are your greatest average ticket and gross margin employees. Don't just throw a low level employee on the register. Put a sales person on the register. You can rotate who's on the register if needed, but don't neglect this vital spot. Not every sales person will engage with every customer, but every customer has to check out, so they will at one point end up at the register. Have a great sales person here. Make them on the top of your priority list for training, you won't regret it.

Closing

The final recommendation I can make is to never lose sight of why you are there. If you're the sales manager or supervisor, that is your job. Other functions may overlap, you may find yourself on a register, or making copies, or hiring. All of these are part of your job, but your main focus should remain on sales. Train one person and let them repeat that training to others. One-on-One produces the best results from my years of experience in sales and food service. Don't waste valuable sales time on pointless training. Keep training short- five minutes is ideal. Have team huddles at the start of a shift, clearly communicate your goals for that day, that week, and beyond. Also lead by example. Make it a point that no matter how busy you are with other things, that you take time to help at least one customer per day. You can boost those sales and profits yourself with 30 customers per month. Your team will see you do it and they will follow in your example.

General HACCP and Food Safety Training
Condensed Safety Training/Refresher/HACCP:

by Joshua R. Embry

Section 1: High Risk Populations:

A chain is only as strong as its weakest link. High risk population groups are the first to get sick or even die when serving questionable or contaminated food. Their immune systems are in a weakened state, making them less able to fight off infection from contaminants such as bacteria.

Who are they? PIES

Pregnant, Infants, Elderly, or people with Systems that are already impaired (think cancer, etc.)

Think about these people with everything we put out. Never take a risk when it comes to safety.

4 main sources of contamination:

Biological, Chemical, Physical, and Cross-contamination.

Bio = living etc. Chemical -think of over-spraying sanitizer right onto someone's food when sanitizing an area. Physical - think of broken glass or metal shards, rocks, etc. Cross-contamination - think of preparing someone's fresh chopped salad right on top of a counter that you just chopped raw bloody chicken on without properly cleaning the area between jobs.

Section 2: Biological Hazards:

Bacteria - produce toxins - can multiply or double every 20 minutes. 1 can become 1 billion in 10-12 hours.

High protein, moisture, time left out, and temperature all aid in growth.

Viruses: microorganisms that do not use food to reproduce. Food is only used as a means of transportation. They can't multiply on their own, they need a living host.

Spread through poor personal hygiene. Wash your hands thoroughly and frequently.

Hepatitis A: Affects the lover, leading cause- poor personal hygiene or hand washing

Norwalk or Norovirus: lives in the human intestinal tract, transmitted through exposure to fecal contamination. Wash your hands!

Parasites- live within or feed off of another host. Can be killed by freezing to a low temp (-4F for 7 days) or cooking at a high enough temp.

Trichinella - found in pork and other wild game.

Fungi - mold and spores

Mostly dangerous because they can cause allergies, especially in high risk populations.

Chemical Hazards:

Cleaners, acids, detergents, degreasers, soaps, chemicals, and pesticides can get into food.

This is one reason we wash produce etc. We should never store any chemicals or cleaners in the same area as food. Notice our cleaners are below the rags on their own shelf. It is never okay to leave chemicals laying around out of this area. Example: don't leave green soap under the cooks counter, put it away after cleaning the tilt.

MSDS- safety binder is located below the spray bottles, if you have a reaction to a chemical, seek help from a coworker, notify management, and check the MSDS on how to treat.

Physical Contamination:
Caused when hair, glass, metal, shavings, shells, bones, or broken objects get into food.

Dangers of Cross-Contamination:
caused when bacteria or other harmful organisms transfer from one place to another. It's the transfer of substances to an unclean to a clean source. Usually from raw meat to ready to eat foods like salad, etc. This is why it's vital that we sanitize and clean the salad prep sink areas after we've thawed meats there.

Properly storing foods helps eliminate this, this is why you hear us telling you if things aren't being stacked correctly in the fridge or freezer. i.e. poultry at the bottom, salad on the top etc.

Section 3: Practicing Personal Hygiene/Hand-washing:

Practicing proper personal hygiene is important to protecting Hartland from foodborne illness. Saliva, sweat, and other bodily fluids can be harmful sources of contamination if they get into food.

Clean clothing and uniforms are required. Wear aprons when working with extra messy items (raw meats, baking, etc.)

Improper food tasting: Harmful germs can be transferred to food when an employee uses their finger or a utensil more than once to taste food.

Smoking -this is easy, Hartland is a smoking-free facility as a term of employment.

Jewelry - only a plain metal band is allowed, and still needs to be cleaned. My recommendation is to take it off and store it somewhere to save time and prevent loss or damage to your ring.

Gloves- treat gloves like your hands, they aren't some magical sanitizing agent, they can get dirty like anything else, change gloves between tasks and wash your hands between glove changes.

In our kitchen, gloves must be worn whenever food is in a finished state and not being cooked further - i.e. mixing salad, running food to the lines, cookies, etc. Also when working with meats or other messy foods. It is best to wear gloves at nearly all times, when in doubt, wear gloves.

CDC Says: 80,000 people per year die from foodborne illness.

Proper Hand washing:
Wet your hands, and use soap on your hands or any part of your arm if exposed. Make sure 10-15 seconds are used for the actual scrubbing. Dry your hands.

Hand sanitizers are not substitutes for hand washing.

Section 4: Purchasing, Receiving, and Storing Food Safely:

We can only purchase from USDA sources - i.e. Sysco and JD Foods, we can't stop at the orange stand down the road etc.

Incoming food must be inspected - when a truck pulls up, look inside of it, reject damaged or soiled goods. Frozen food should arrive at 0F or less, cold food should be received at 40F or less, and hot food received at 135F or higher (140F for us).

Food must be stored on shelves at least 6 inches off of the ground. It is never acceptable to leave food directly on the ground.

Meats should look and smell fresh - you want red beef, and avoid darkened wing tips and soft or sticky flesh in poultry. Packaged foods should be checked for cracks, punctures, dents, or leaks.

Eggs and milk-based products are considered a potentially hazardous foods and must be put away promptly.

Produce, wash before serving. If possible, cut away bruised or damaged areas since bacteria can grow well in these areas.

Cooling foods: The first stage is to get the food down to 70F within 2 hours. The second stage is getting the food from 70F to below 41F within an additional 4 hours.

Methods:

Stir food, Smaller portions, Shallow pans, Ice wand/stick, Ice bath, Using ice directly.

Section 5: Equipment and Utensils:

Food contact surfaces must be easy to clean and sanitize. All food contact and equipment surfaces should be cleaned at least every 4 hours if in continuous use.

Section 6: Preparing, Cooking, and Serving Food Safely:

Never use glass or mercury filled thermometers. The temp dial must read from 0F-220F. Thermometers must be at least 5 inches in length. They must be accurate within +/- 2F. They can be calibrated at 32F or 212F (32F is freezing, crushed ice and water, 212F is boiling water).

Thawing:

frozen food must be thawed properly.

CROW:

Cooking, **R**efrigeration, **O**ven, **W**ater (Cold Running) - you can cook from frozen - as in the tilt skillet or in a pot on the stove, thaw from moving from the freezer into fridge, thaw while baking directly from frozen in the oven, or running under cold continuously flowing water.

Internal Cooking Temperatures:

Poultry (Chicken/Turkey) or reheated foods: **165F** for at least 15 seconds (also ground poultry)

All ground meats including ground pork and ground fish: **165F** for at least 15 seconds (our temp)

(Federal foodsafety.org says 160F, ServSafe Says 155F)

Whole Pork, Lamb, Beef, and fish: **145F**

Allergies: 12 million + people have a foodborne allergy in the United States.

Each year at least 150 people die in America from food allergies. 30,000 people seek emergency food allergy treatment each year.
Anaphylactic shock: can include - hives, tightness of throat, itching, swelling, and death.
Eight major food allergens are:
Milk, Eggs, Fish, Shellfish, Nuts from trees, Soybeans, Wheat, and Peanuts.

Section 7: Cleaning and Sanitizing:

Cleanliness is one of the top considerations when choosing a place to eat. This centers around 2 main principles:
Cleaning: the removal of food particles and residue from surfaces that have come into contact with food
Sanitizing: after cleaning, surfaces must be treated with hot water of chemicals to reduce contaminants to safe levels. Sanitizing is the treatment of a surface previously cleaned to reduce the # of disease-causing microorganisms to safe levels.
3 approved chemical sanitizers (ICQ)
Iodine, Chlorine, or Quaternary Ammonium Compounds (Quats)
Machine dishwashers: low temp machines like we have, should be around 1200F to be most effective at dislodging foods, but the sanitization occurs from the chemicals we add. high temp machines rely on a combination of superheated water and chemicals.

Section 8: Facility Safety

Health inspections:
Make sure the inspector identifies themselves with proper identification.
Keep the relationship professional
Do not take it personally if you receive one or more violations.

Illumination - lighting should have protective fixtures to prevent shattering and physical contamination.
Pay attention to backflow - this is talking about sinks - don't set things down into sinks where dirty water can backflow up and into your foods. Avoid using the sink closest to the baker area for this reason in regards to straining etc. as it backflows often.
Indoor trashcans: must be leak and waterproof, covered (bags), and emptied as needed
Outside trashcans: durable, non-absorbent, leak-proof, insect and rodent-resistant ,and kept clean.
This means spraying it out if it's got nastiness in it.

Pests:
3 most common are mice, rats, and roaches.
Best method is prevention, seal up holes and cracks, leave your facility clean - pickup spills and don't leave easily accessible foods out.
We use the baker's clear case to help with this and we should have clean counters and floors before leaving.

We also use roach bait traps and mouse traps - to be checked and replaced as needed. If you ever see a tripped mouse trap that is empty, wear gloves and reset it, then toss the gloves and wash your hands really well.

Section 9: Best Practices:
Once food is properly cooked or stored, it's important to prevent contamination in the final stages. Never touch main areas of plates, cups, or utensils, hold dishes from the bottom or the edge.
Never stack wet dishes - we store bowls upside down etc. to prevent water buildup etc.
Use tongs or utensils to serve ready to eat foods like salad or muffins etc.
Use an ice scoop to get ice.

Employees learn best by active participation:
This means we give you one-on-one training and from a variety of tools like job aids, posters, and employee guides.

Illness:
There are times when it is appropriate not to come into work. These times don't include general fatigue where you may have stayed up too late the night before, headaches, or a general "blah" feeling. Appropriate times are when you have a fever- measured by a thermometer - not a gut feeling, or visible abrasions like a sever rash, or pink-eye-ness. Vomiting (other than from food intolerances, don't say you're sick when you're lactose intolerant and decide to down a milkshake.) is generally a time not to come in. You can always ask your management team for clarification. If you aren't feeling well and/or are having diarrhea or stomach issues, wash your hands extremely well - whether you meet the criteria to stay home or remain at work.
There may be a time when the flu hits an entire camp and ALL people on the hill are ill, at those times check with management. This doesn't often occur but it has in the past and people still need to eat.
At all times, call management to notify them if you are going to be absent and be aware that a doctor's note may be required to return to work. If you do stay home sick, don't abuse sick time as a time to run errands down the hill or take trips. If you're too sick to work, you should be confined to your housing unless visiting a Dr. and returning with a note. Sick leave abuse will not be tolerated.

Complete Kitchen Safety Training with Safety Sign-off Sheets for:

Griddle/Flat Tops/Tilts, Convection/Non-Convection Ovens, Dish machines, Free Standing and Counter-Top Mixers, Refrigerator/Freezer Training, Meat Slicer Safety, and Stove-tops

by Joshua R. Embry

Below you will find specific training for all listed kitchen equipment. At the end of the booklet you will find each of the sign-off forms that you can add to your HACCP Binder. A general fill-in form(not in this book) will also be available online at http://www.embryinc.com/food/safety if you would prefer to keep a single safety sign-off form on file that you can simply write in the course name for. If you'd like to purchase our Condensed HACCP Food Safety Training Guide that deals with general food safety from Amazon you can do so here.

Tip: use section 7 of each training to recap items your team may be missing.

Please note that depending on your reading device (Kindle, PC, etc.) some pages may not align properly. You can access the sign-off sheets online in an easier to print medium. You also have permission to copy and print the sign-off sheets for future use - only if you've purchased this book. This does not grant permission to republish or distribute.

Safety Training

Dish Machine Cleaning, Usage, and Safety

The Dish Machine has the potential to cause great harm to you or others if not used in accordance with proper maintenance, assembly, careful attention, and cleanliness.

This course will focus on all of the above.

By signing off on this course, you agree to have participated in this training and have a firm grasp on each of its segments.

Safety is our goal.

Step 1: Proper Assembly

(Ensure all pipes are connected, all catches, hoses are tight, etc.) If you see loose or damaged connections, report to your management immediately.

Step 2: Ensure Safety Measures are in place

(Check Chemical and temp levels PRIOR to use) This means verifying your sanitizer buckets have chemical in them and that the machine is dispersing them correctly. You can use test strips to determine this. See your user manual to determine the type of test strip needed.

Step 3: Pay attention, clear distractions

(Hot water, Chemicals, Wet Surfaces/Floor) The floor may be wet and hazardous. Seek out non-slip mats if possible and clean up spills as they occur.

Step 4: Proper Usage

(Don't put people/animals through the machine or non-food service objects)

This may seem like a joke, but multiple institutions have seen this type of horseplay happen.

Step 5: Disassembly

(Clear all traps, spray out machine etc.)

Your specific machine will have anywhere from 1-5 "Traps" it uses to collect and filter solids. One is usually on your spray counter, the others are generally screen cylinders that are found where your water drains from your machine (either internal or external to the machine) and there can often be an additional metal filter found at the base of your machine with a slide out tray. Ensure these are all empty to avoid odor and insect/rodent interest in your food service operation.

Step 6: Proper Cleaning and Storage

(Clean machine inside and out, clean counters, clean floor, put dishes away, etc.)

The outside of your machine must remain clean. Wipe the top and sides of the machine often. Keep the entire work surface clean. This also includes the clean-side of the dish machine where clean dishes exit. Food particles here can still present a health and safety issue.

Step 7: Recap with your team.

Step 8: Q&A

Does your team have any questions?

Safety Training

Free-Standing and Counter-Top Mixer Cleaning, Usage, and Safety

The Free Standing and Counter-Top Mixers have the potential to cause great harm to you or others if not used in accordance with proper maintenance, assembly, careful attention, and cleanliness.

This course will focus on all of the above.

By signing off on this course, you agree to have participated in this training and have a firm grasp on each of its segments.

Safety is our goal.

Step 1: Proper Assembly

(Never swap parts while machine is running, go over different attachments)

Avoid the temptation of reaching in too soon. Allow the machine to come to a complete stop before reaching in.

Step 2: Ensure Safety Measures are in place

(No loose clothing, no necklaces/wallet chains, untied aprons, no spatulas left in mixer, etc.)

Many machines have safety measures that include a guard or kill switch if the bowl is not in the proper position. Refer to your user manual if you are unfamiliar with them.

Step 3: Pay attention, clear distractions

(Stand away from machine if you are changing tasks, don't lean on the machine)

Many employees have tried to use the machine to lean on while working, some have learned the hard way that it only takes one article of loose clothing or an apron to cause severe injury. Don't forget to take your spatulas and spoons out of the bowl before turning it on as they can be thrown from the machine or broken up into your food.

Step 4: Proper Usage

Never add ingredients while the machine is running. Stop the machine, add ingredients, then continue operation. Initial usage will require the installation of the mixing bowl. Line the bowl up with any safety devices, usually including two forward pegs that are located on either side and which the mixing bowl has receiving holes predrilled. There is often also an additional safety lip on the mixer and bowl that will line up towards the back of the mixing bowl. These items ensure the bowl will stay securely fastened during use and help prevent injury. With the bowl installed add your initial ingredients then add your mixing device (paddle, whisk, dough hook, etc.) , with applicable machines, use the lifting arm to raise the level of the bowl. Select your operating speed (usually #1 to start), ensure any safety devices are attached correctly and that any measuring devices or spatulas are no longer in the mixing bowl. Ensure no loose clothing or other items have become tangled in the equipment and start the machine.

Step 5: Disassembly

(Turn machine OFF before removing parts, etc.)

Most mixers use a lift and twist approach to remove attachments. Look at the top and side of the attachment to see the grooves. Turn and lift to safely dislodge, then lower into the bowl for removal.

Step 6: Proper Cleaning and Storage

(Remove all parts, wash in Dish room, put away, clean backsplash of mixer, entire surface, floor, underside of mixer -

where the hooks attach, items are splashed, buttons, handles, footing, items near mixer such as walls or storage bins, etc.)

Never leave your mixer dirty. This leads to cross contamination. It's often easiest to clean the mess real time rather than wait.

Step 7: Recap Key Issues

Step 8: Q&A

Does your team have any questions?

Safety Training

<u>Convection/Non-Convection Oven Cleaning, Usage, and Safety</u>

The Convection/Non-Convection Ovens have the potential to cause great harm to you or others if not used in accordance with proper maintenance, assembly, careful attention, and cleanliness.

This course will focus on all of the above.

By signing off on this course, you agree to have participated in this training and have a firm grasp on each of its segments.

Safety is our goal.

Step 1: Proper Assembly

(Racks, Fan Assembly Housing, etc.)

Each oven is slightly different but has similar components. Convection fans often have a shield in place to prevent items from banging directly into them. Foil can often get caught in here and ruin your fan or motor. Ensure you do not hear and scraping or odd sounds coming from your oven. If you do, unplug the device, remove racks and the safety shield (usually 5-6 wing nut screws) and dislodge any foil you may see. Reattach and plug your unit back in and test for successful operation.

Step 2: Ensure Safety Measures are in place

(Ensure pilot is lit, Use hot pads, avoid hot surfaces/doors)

Make sure your oven is set up the way you need it before using it. Are the racks spaced far enough apart for the items you'll be cooking? Visibly check your pilot light to ensure it is lit. Pilot lights are often found on the bottom section of the oven where there is a removable shield in place. You can either remove this shield by pulling (no tools required) or by leaning below it and looking up to see a flame.

Step 3: Pay attention, clear distractions

(Grease splashing from food pans, hot food, wet floor, grease on floor, others walking by, open oven doors, etc.)

Ovens are hot, you will likely get burns from time to time. Remember to use correct lifting techniques and hot pads to prevent injury. Don't panic if you are suffering from a minor burn while removing an item. If it's not possible to safely put it back in place to start again, do not throw or drop the pan as it could result in greater injury as the entire content can splash on you. Have a plan in place as to where you are going to place hot items before you pull them out.

Step 4: Proper Usage

Do not misuse ovens. This can include melting non-food items, thawing or warming clothing, and more. Ovens are for food only. Ensure your racks are set with the correct clearance for the items you wish to cook. Ensure the pilot light is lit and the correct temperature settings are in place. Insert cooking pans as desired. Close the door and if convection, turn on fan. Set a timer to keep track of your cook times and prevent oven fires.

Step 5: Disassembly

(Removal of racks, removal of fan housing)

Typical disassembly of units involves individual racks that items are cooked on as well as side holders that these slide into. Both must be remove to adequately clean the oven.

Step 6: Proper Cleaning and Storage

(Clean spills with a thick damp towel, use dough cutter as a scraper, salt can stop burning spills in a pinch, wipe outside and inside of doors, scrip racks)

Spills can lead to fires or a kitchen filled with smoke. In the moment if cleaning isn't possible salt can be tossed onto a spill to neutralize smoke and odor. Once the cooking process is complete this must be scrapped out and cleaned prior to operation again.

Step 7: Recap Key items

Step 8: Q&A

Does your team have any questions?

Safety Training

Fridge and Freezer, Usage, and Safety

The Fridge and Freezer have the potential to cause great harm to you or others if not used in accordance with proper maintenance, assembly, careful attention, and cleanliness.

This course will focus on all of the above.

By signing off on this course, you agree to have participated in this training and have a firm grasp on each of its segments.

Safety is our goal.

Step 1: Proper Assembly

(Ensure all racks are firm and stable before storing, ensure freezer safety exit bar is working)

Do not store food on loose racks or shelves as it can fall and injure you or contaminate other foods.

Step 2: Ensure Safety Measures are in place

(Ensure no leaking food or containers, food stored properly, all date labels are present, etc.)

Food must be stored in containers or on trays that will prevent leaking and contamination of other foods. Foods must also be stored in the correct order. See your HACCP binder for details, in general meats must be on the bottom, starches above those, then vegetables at the very top.

Step 3: Pay attention, clear distractions

(Water, Chemicals, Wet Surfaces/Floor)

Condensation or spills can create slippery environments. Be aware of where you are walking and clean up any spills promptly.

Step 4: Proper Usage

(Store food in proper configuration and containers)

Store only certified and inspected foods in your units. Brining in outside items increases the likelihood of cross contamination or introducing foreign objects into your operation. Do not store personal food in the same unit as your operational foods.

Step 5: Disassembly

(Remove rolling racks, items when cleaning, etc.)

Empty any portable racks from the unit before sweeping or mopping to ensure adequate cleaning has been performed.

Step 6: Proper Cleaning and Storage

(Mop fridge, wipe shelves, clean spills as they occur, never leave spills on containers, sweep freezer only, etc.)

Step 7: Recap Key items

Step 8: Q&A

Does your team have any questions?

Safety Training

<u>Meat Slicer Safety, Operation, Cleaning, and Storage</u>

The meat slicer has the potential to cause great harm to you or others if not used in accordance with proper maintenance, assembly, careful attention, and cleanliness.

This course will focus on all of the above.

By signing off on this course, you agree to have participated in this training and have a firm grasp on each of its segments.

Safety is our goal.

Step 1: Proper Assembly

Meat slicers have protective gear in place that must be attached correctly before operation. This usually includes a blade cover and handle attachment for pushing meats forward in slicing. When not in use a blade cover should also be attached. Use of a cutting glove is recommended but may not be required at all locations. Check your local safety ordinances for specifics.

Step 2: Ensure Safety Measures are in place

Once assembled, power on the slicer and do a blank test run. If you hear grinding or other noises, turn the machine off, disassemble and try again. Improper assembly or lack of safety guards can lead to metal shavings ending up in your food or personal injury.

Step 3: Pay attention, clear distractions

Do not talk with others while using the meat slicer. Focus on the task at hand and turn the machine off and step away if you must speak with another person.

Step 4: Proper Usage

The meat slicer is for food use only, do not attempt to cut other materials with it. Once safely assembled you may begin preparing your items. Only use the machine if you have been trained on and feel comfortable using it. Never take shortcuts and take a break if you become fatigued. Do not misuse safety devices. Once the meat or items is secured set the desired thickness via the control knob. Test slice by pushing the item forward via the slicing arm. Verify correct thickness or make modifications to size as needed. Repeat as needed.

Step 5: Disassembly

Unplug the machine before taking it apart. Keep in mind there are sharp objects. Take your time and be safe. Clean all surfaces.

Step 6: Proper Cleaning and Storage

All surfaces must be clean, this includes the outside casing of the machine as well as underneath it where food and blood can get lodged. Always finish with sanitizer.

Step 7: Recap Key items

Step 8: Q&A

Does your team have any questions?

Safety Training

<u>Stove-Top Cleaning, Usage, and Safety</u>

The Stove-Top has the potential to cause great harm to you or others if not used in accordance with proper maintenance, assembly, careful attention, and cleanliness.

This course will focus on all of the above.

By signing off on this course, you agree to have participated in this training and have a firm grasp on each of its segments.

Safety is our goal.

Step 1: Proper Assembly

(Ensure all igniters and cast iron pieces are in place)

Visually check your equipment to make sure there are no obvious safety issues prior to operation. The cast iron pieces are what sit on top and should be level and in place. This will prevent heavy pots from spilling over. The igniters are what the cooking flame comes out of. They often just get pushed onto a fitting near the handles you use to turn the stove are located. If they aren't lined up correctly you could end up with flames in areas you wouldn't prefer. They often can get out of alignment when the stove has recently been deep cleaned and they may have been removed. When you turn the gas on for a burner you shouldn't hear a rushing air noise anywhere except where the gas should be coming out. If you do, remove and reinstall this piece.

Step 2: Ensure Safety Measures are in place

(Ensure pilot lights are on, no hissing gas sounds)

Pilot lights need to be lit at all times. If they are not you could end up with a buildup of gas, especially overnight when the hood systems may be off.

Step 3: Pay attention, clear distractions

(Fire, Grease, and Steam can all be present)

Never leave items unattended on the stove. This doesn't mean you can't temporarily walk away from boiling water, but it does mean you don't want to leave grease or butter on by itself as they have a higher probability of catching fire.

Step 4: Proper Usage

(Watch what you cook, don't leave grease, etc. unattended)

Again, you must monitor what you are cooking to prevent unnecessary hazards from jeopardizing the safety of your team and guests. Utilize a double boiler method for delicate sauces or long-term cooking items. Never use water to put out a grease fire. You can use flour or a fire extinguisher to do this. Never try to move a fire, leave it in place and work to extinguish it in place. Spilling a grease fire can injure you and spread the fire across your kitchen, it is always best to leave it in place where safety measures are already in place to prevent it's spread. It will eventually burn itself out.

Step 5: Disassembly

(Remove stained surface or gas channels when needed, etc.)

Be mindful that even if not in use some parts will be hot to the touch due to the pilot lights. Always use hot pads or rags when taking the stovetop apart. Start with the top metal that your pans rest on. Then remove the igniters (the parts that the cooking gas comes out of, aka burners. Clean all remaining surfaces then remove the drip tray. Usually a thin tray exists underneath the burners and can be slid out. Clean the area this rested on and wash all components you have removed. Reassemble in reverse order.

Step 6: Proper Cleaning and Storage

(clean spills promptly or after usage, use caution as surface can remain hot for long periods of time, clean bottom grease trap and/or replace foil often, etc.)

A metal scrubber will work well with hard metal surfaces but may scratch shiny surfaces. Scrub all burners, igniters, and other components. Don't forget to clean the face/front of your equipment and the handles.

Step 7: Recap Key items

Step 8: Q&A

Does your team have any questions?

Safety Training

Tilt Skillet & Griddle Cleaning, Usage, and Safety

The tilt skillet & griddle have the potential to cause great harm to you or others if not used in accordance with proper maintenance, assembly, careful attention, and cleanliness.

This course will focus on all of the above.

By signing off on this course, you agree to have participated in this training and have a firm grasp on each of its segments.

Safety is our goal.

Step 1: Proper Assembly

(when applicable/grease trap in place for griddle, etc.)

Ensure your cook-top is fully attached and level as some can be removed for cleaning. Apply a thin coat of oil on the cooking surface to prevent rust between use and to enhance the cooking efficiency and longevity of your equipment.

Step 2: Ensure Safety Measures are in place

(Tilt in lowered position before use)

If your device can tilt, ensure it is in the cooking position prior to turning it on. Many devices have safety switches in place to prevent this but older equipment often lacks this kind of safety measure. Also ensure that all surfaces including the underside of the lid are clean prior to use to prevent cross contamination.

Step 3: Pay attention, clear distractions

(Grease splashing, unattended food can burn/catch fire, etc.)

This is a hot cooking surface and can cause harm to you or others if you are not attentive when using it. Water coming into contact with grease or oil can result in flare ups or grease burns. Ensure your equipment is free of water before use (unless boiling water etc.).

Step 4: Proper Usage

Do not use tilts or griddles to melt non-food items. Ensure a clean surface exists prior to use and clean promptly after each use. To being, apply a layer of non-stick coating (oil or spray). Turn your equipment to the proper cooking temperature (often 350F or higher). Ensure your work station is clean before cooking and plan ahead with pans or other ways to store your food once cooking is complete.

Step 5: Disassembly

(Clear Grease trap, etc.)

Most equipment comes with a grease trap that will capture unused grease or water and debris from cleaning. This can become a hotspot for bacteria. Be sure to empty this after every use and wash at least weekly if not at all times.

Step 6: Proper Cleaning and Storage

(Clean inner and outer lid, all lips, for tilt underneath cooking surface, sides, facing, floor around, etc.)

Be sure to clean all sides of your equipment as well as any items that may have fallen underneath it as unattended food debris can lead to rodent or insect infestations. Water and other liquids left on the ground around or underneath can also create a slipping hazard for you and your team.

Step 7: Recap Key items

Step 8: Q&A

Does your team have any questions?

Convection(/Non) Oven Safety Sign-Off Sheet
(Sign/Date)

Dish Machine Sign-Off Sheet (Sign/Date)

Mixer Sign-Off Sheet (Sign/Date)

Fridge & Freezer Sign-Off Sheet (Sign/Date)

Meat Slicer Sign-Off Sheet (Sign/Date)

Stove-Top Sign-Off Sheet (Sign/Date)

Tilt Skillet/Griddle Sign-Off Sheet (Sign/Date)

Battling Perception

The reality behind customer service and the dreaded survey

By Joshua Embry

Perception, what you're *actually* graded on. In the customer service world many businesses have shifted to an extreme focus on customer surveys. It makes sense, you want your customers to return and make purchases, and there's nothing wrong with the goal. Where it can get tricky is determining the line between fact and customer perception. Did it really take them 45 minutes to get their french fries? Was your store really the filthiest place they've ever been to? Maybe, but not likely. When reviewing surveys and customer comments you have to take away the very reasonable response of getting defensive. What the customer is rating is simply their perception of what happened, it doesn't mean that it's true.

Let's take a look at some familiar negative customer survey responses:

What the customer says vs. what was likely the case
It was too expensive | It cost more than I was expecting to pay, I didn't see the value in it
It took forever | I had a different expectation of time, I was busy, I was in a hurry
They were so rude | They didn't give me what I wanted, even if it wasn't policy or reasonable
I'm going to corporate! | I'm going to keep complaining until I feel heard, or… I want something
You should fix this | I bought it from you so you must be the one who makes it and warranty it

These are likely the most common responses that you see. Responses can vary as some systems of measurement are based on numbers.   A normal example that we see is 1-5 with 5 being the highest and 1 being the lowest. The scale can change but the customer is ultimately being asked if they were satisfied with the level or quality of service that they received, and that can be tricky as every customer can have a different perception of how things should have gone. One customer would be thrilled with the interaction, another could have viewed the same service as subpar.

Welcome to the world of customer service. What you need to realize right now is that you're not being measured on what you actually do in reality. You're being measured on what you do in perception.

Let's look at some case studies that have actually occurred in my experience.
Company X provides cellular phone service. The customer, let's call them John, is having an issue with his phone. He's calling in and is within the return period for the phone.
The phone specialist checks the network and sees there is no issue with the cell towers or the customer's account, after some light troubleshooting it is determined that the phone is having

issues. The specialist offers to exchange or return the phone since the customer is within the company's return policy. The customer accepts and orders an alternate phone. While there was an issue, the customer left feeling that things were handled. He may have a negative perception of the phone now, but his phone service company came through. Some background information is that the phone service provider doesn't actually manufacture the phones, they have to buy them from the manufacturer then resell them. The manufacturer in turn agrees to exchange or refund defective devices within a certain time frame. After that time frame the customer must work with the manufacturer directly. This is normal in the telecom industry.

In the same scenario, let's change the fact that the customer was within return guidelines and now let's say they are 6 months into having this phone. Again, the specialist determines there are no network or account issues and troubleshooting has determined it is again a phone issue. The specialist advises the customer that they can work with the manufacturer as the device is still within the 1 year manufacturer warranty. They even offer to transfer them over to make the process as simple as possible. The customer perception is now at play.

Regardless of the reality of the situation, the customer wants their phone replaced, and they want it now. They don't want to wait for a manufacturer to fulfill the warranty by mailing in their old device and waiting for a new one. After all, he's paying his bill monthly, that means his provider should replace his phone when it breaks...right? When the specialist advises the customer of their options and even after a supervisor has been engaged and the customer has been given clear expectations they ultimately provide the lowest score on a survey.

There are multiple principles at play here, one is the customer's understanding of how your business actually works. Their perception is that your company makes lots of money off of their service. In reality they don't understand that there are costs associated with maintaining their service, paying staff, keeping the lights on, repairing those multi-million dollar cell phone towers, repairing or upgrading network equipment to keep up with industry standards, and so much more. The customer imagines a room or warehouse full of phones that you could just send them at the click of a button, not understanding that most phones are direct shipped from the manufacturer, or shipped in batches and quickly distributed to various sales channels. He doesn't understand that you're at a call center and there are literally zero phones for sale there. The perception of the customer is that you CAN do something and that you are CHOOSING not to do it. Surely someone can do something, right? In some cases yes, but likely they won't like the option to take it to a repair center or receive a refurbished model. Again, the perception is that you CAN do something and you WON'T.

This is just one example, you don't need me to list 50 case studies broken down by demographic and geographic location. You don't need to hear that common perceptions from New York customers differ from customers in Nebraska with the same issues. You don't need me to tell you about personality types and how they interact with you. You've seen multiple scenarios, you know the outcomes. We're not focusing on every psychological detail as to why they have the perception or why they throw you under a bus in a survey, but how to prevent it and how to reduce those occurrences in the future.

Perception is much deeper than you initially think. It comes from preconceived notions from a variety of places including past experiences, childhood, environmental conditions, family history, work experience, and peer pressures. It permeates every part of society and it's not going away.

Perception is how your spouse thinks you looked at them or that "tone" they hear in your voice. Let's face it, sometimes their perception is right! Sometimes it's not. So don't expect to be able to change someone's perception if you're purposefully trying to distort reality.

We're working with customer perception that differs from reality in this book. If you got slammed on a survey and you truly have the filthiest store in the state, grab a mop and scrubbers and get to work. There is no magical perception wand that can skew reality into your mythical favor, so don't waste your time. If a customer provides honest feedback that is true and you can change it, then do so.

Where it becomes more complicated is when you look at the feedback on a survey and it doesn't match the reality of what is seen. It's even more complicated when it matches what you see and there is nothing you can do about it.

If your company's policy is preventing the resolution the customer wants, there's not much you can do. You can pitch the options again, and you can even go above and beyond in simplifying those options. In the end you're going to continue to get hit in those areas on surveys and your company knows it, but they've determined (at least for now) that the negative perception is worth it in the end. This could be because the solution would be too costly on a large scale or because they don't believe it's a true issue. Either way, expect more of the same.

Let's focus on customer perceptions that are way off base and how to bring them closer to reality. If you're calling a customer back that means you've already received the survey. Your best option here is to call them back with options available, review their issue before you call them back so you don't waste time. Often just knowing the issue and being prepared for the call is perceived by the customer in a positive way. Their perception is that they've been heard and you are working to fix the issue.

A better avenue compared to reactive response is a proactive response. So you've failed to meet one customer's expectations based on their perception. You work to resolve that customer's issues but then you look ahead on an ongoing basis. What could have changed or been done differently to prevent that perception in the first place, use this for your other customers.

Again, if your survey provides you with a real issue that can be fixed, do it. Is your bathroom in disrepair? You can paint it, clean it, replace broken paper towel dispensers, paint over the obscene pictures someone tagged in the bathroom stall, and have employees check it's cleanliness every hour. Paint is often less than $10/gallon and restrooms are the smallest rooms in your building. What you can't change is the customer that expects you to have marble countertops and a bathroom attendant in your office supply store.

One of the best ways you can impact customer perception is by providing an overall positive experience. If you're polite, have clean appearance, and are helpful they will likely see you that way, even if an issue comes up. This will result in a customer marking a 3 on a 1-5 scale instead of a 1 when they have a real issue. You may be thinking that 3 is still unacceptable, but relative to a 1, you're doing pretty well. We're not talking about making all of your customer surveys a 3 here, we're talking about moving as many of your lowest rated surveys up to the midrange. Why would you want to do that? Your surveys total average is a key metric that can show you what's really happening in your store or location.

If you have 10 total surveys and 2 of them are rated as 1, 3 rated at 3, and 5 rated at 5. That's 1+1+3+3+3+5+5+5+5+5 = 36. 36 total survey points divided by 10 surveys means your average customer survey is 3.6 out of 5.

Let's move those scores that were rated as a 1 up to a rating of 3. So 3+3+3+3+3+5+5+5+5+5= 40 total survey points. Now your average customer survey is 4 out of 5. That's much better and means you're not only meeting customer expectations, but also exceeding them.

You're going to have some low survey scores. The reason is that it is not possible to change every single customer's perception. Do a quick google search on the number of people in your country on medication for depression or mental disorders, alternately how many people are divorced, how many are currently in therapy, it's not a small number. And while I'm not saying everyone who gives you a 1 has a mental disorder or suffers from depression, I am saying that even if you provided the best customer service in the world, you're going to have at some point a customer that is going to rate you poorly based not on what you did but on some external force that you can't control.

The simplest example here was a survey I had received with the lowest scores across the board. The guest had previously had a stroke and had thought the number 1 was the highest score and so they thought they were giving rave reviews. Not every customer understands your rating system and there are chances for human error on their part.
The only way to overcome the negative is to *focus on the customers that you can help with perception*. The number of good surveys will far outweigh the negative or low rated surveys if you're doing everything right.

So how do you change a customer's perception? Initially it's going to be with your first interaction. Whether you're providing phone support or face to face contact, your customer needs to see that you are attentive to their needs and wanting to help. Customers can tell when you're not making eye contact and asking if you can help them. You could be stocking or facing product in your store, continuing in your work while casually asking if they need help. Their perception is that you're busy and often even if they needed help they don't want to interrupt you. Be sure that you are sincere in your offering of assistance and make eye contact if possible. Start your interaction with a smile, and yes smiles can he "heard" over the phone.

If you're in a service environment, let's say in a restaurant, perception is going to be a high priority. There's a delicate balance of asking your guest if everything is going well every minute or when they have food in their mouth, or are in the middle of a drink or active conversation. The perception here is negative, you're bugging them! In reality you're working really hard to make sure they're doing well because you want a nice tip or survey, but you may be working too hard at it. Your customer interaction needs to feel natural, not robotic. The other end of the scale is the waitress that seats you then disappears into the abyss. You look around, the restaurant doesn't seem that busy, but you're scrambling to ask busboys for help. You can't believe how rude your server is by not serving you, you've waited what seems like forever and you don't even have your drinks yet! Or, you've had great service from when you walked in until now...right now you've been sitting at your meal with an empty beverage glass, it's been forever. You've noticed because the two different times you want to take a drink, your cup was empty. Where's the customer service? Yes, she took your order and got your delicious food to you promptly, but then she abandoned you. How dare she smile and talk with another employee when you're cup is empty. She just doesn't care!

Do you see the perceptions here? What if she was on a break and her coworker Jane was supposed to be watching her tables? Sure she could have let you know that, that would have modified your perception. What if your section was slow, but the server was serving another section out of your site that had 10 full tables! None of that matters to the customer what matters is what *they* experience. So again, what can you do here? Manage your time and set clear expectations. Let them know you're a little short staffed and are covering another section but that you'll be with them as soon as you can. Bribe your busboy with some shared tips if he'll help keep an eye on and/or get drinks for your guests if you're swamped. Let your manager know that you're a little swamped and that it would really help that customer survey out if he took them their drinks and checked in on them for you. And smiles, smiles all around. Don't avoid eye contact with your guests, don't ignore them. Sometimes a simple nod and wave let's them know you have seen them and their need and are going to be helping them in a moment. Compliment them if appropriate. Do you like their sweater, mention it. Again, look at appropriateness, if it's a low-cut see through top you might be sending the wrong signal. Does it look like they've just come from the salon? Compliment their hair. Do you know about the sports team on their hat? Engage them. It can be short, but these are the small things you can do to impact the customer's perception. If you're an over the phone specialist, notice their location. "Oh Florida! I've always wanted to visit there, how's the weather?" It shows them that you're more than a voice on the other end of the phone, you're a person. Keep it short and professional but throw in a couple of personal connections along the way.

If your customer asks you a question like how you're doing, share a little. Don't spend minutes and hours talking about the world, they called for a reason, or they came into your restaurant for a reason, but it is okay to share a positive life event. If the customer asks how your day is going, it's okay to say you just got engaged! Then ask how their day is going. It's okay to tell the customer that you're just getting back from having your first baby or back from a trip or that it's your Friday! It's exciting and engaging, just don't live in that moment. Open up a small aspect of your world, and only positive. This engages the customer on a personal level. Do this too much and it will be a negative, do it just right and you're going to get the best tips or surveys you've ever seen.

By engaging your customer in this way, you've immediately changed their perception of the situation. You're no longer the restaurant you work at, the phone company, the salesman. You're a real person, and it's harder to throw a real person under the bus than a big business in a survey. Let's get something straight, you need to serve your customers well, we're talking about what you can do beyond that to help battle any additional perceptions that they bring to the table.

Let's talk about consumer confidence. I touch on this in another book I've written but we'll explore the concept here as well.

Consumer confidence is essentially your customer's perception of value for a product or service and that they're making the right purchasing decision based on those factors. What you can do to aid in this area is to be the pro.

It's hard to fake being a pro, so don't try. You might be new at a job but you can read a spec sheet and stall while you find the answer. This works some of the time, but to really be a pro that can build consumer confidence you have to know about your product. Take time during the slow times to learn a little something about what you sell. What features do different printers have, what sets that product apart from another? Once while working at OfficeMax, I did this so well that it almost got me a free trip to Africa. A customer was buying a couple thousand dollars of electronics and through probing I found out she was leading a team going to Africa. Before the end of the sale was over she was saying maybe I should go with their team. An no, it wasn't a cult, and she wasn't hitting on me. She legitimately didn't know much about electronics and saw value in having someone who was a pro there incase things weren't working properly. She was trying to persuade me to join their team, all expenses paid and pay for a 3 month business trip because she didn't have anyone on her team with the technical know-how if a problem should come up. Don't expect to be offered this, but this is what happened to me. I took a few minutes each day and learned a little about the main items that we sold so I could be knowledgeable about them and make recommendations based on the customer's needs. Similar scenarios happened again and again with job offers from customers who saw value in my customer service and technical knowledge. Their perception was that I was a great employee with valuable skills. If surveyed, I was praised. Lesson: Don't fake it.
The customers felt comfortable with my recommendations because of that perception and it built up their consumer confidence. They also became regular customers in my store.

This flows across industry. If you're phone support then learn about your product specs. The nice thing for you is that you've got a computer screen right there to do it. Sales teams in a store environment are often stuck with what's on the box or in a manufacturer-provided hand out. I used to research products online when I got home as it improved my knowledge. A number of manufacturers offer sales training through their websites. Ask your rep next time they come to check your planogram setup or product placement. Often times you can win prizes or receive other compensation for completing online trainings of their products. This is free sales training that I wouldn't pass up.

So far you've learned to engage your customer, add a personal touch, and to build their consumer confidence by learning more about the products and services that you provide. Often times if you hit on 2 out of 3 of these, you'll do well at providing a positive perception to your customer. If you hit all 3 then it's time to move up the ladder.

The Metric Game

By Joshua Embry

The purpose of this booklet is to get you thinking differently about metrics. You may not subscribe to all of the examples listed and may not fully buy-in to these views, and that's okay. If you can, after reading these pages, walk away and begin to really analyze both what and why you're measuring, then it's been a success.

In any number of great books you'll read about the importance of the questions you ask your customers in a survey or about key metrics that will determine if you succeed or fail. Models are developed to forecast the future based on this information. Entire corporate structures and civilizations are built and ultimately destroyed by these faulty metrics.

Has your enterprise bottomed out? Are you just starting out and looking at what to implement early on to ensure your success?

Having worked in Sales Management for OfficeMax Inc., customer service, escalations, technical support, and Quality Assurance for Sprint Nextel, and over a decade in the Food Service industry, I've got to set one thing straight...

Most, if not all, metrics are a waste of time and resources. You cannot quantify the human interaction of relationships the same way you can inventory or revenue.

Let's begin by looking at what is typically being measured:

Call length/Guest interaction length/Time to Resolve.

Issue Resolved

Saved/Retained

At Risk

Customer "Satisfaction"

Will Recommend to Others

Repeat Customer/Rewards Program

Will you Return

There is ultimately one question that really matters to the success of your business.

Are your customers going to come back?

Business rises and falls on this simple principle. Hours of training and billions of dollars are spent on sales and frontline specialists to ensure that your customers will return. Other, less effective sales cultures focus on one-shot-wonders. They desire to increase that current sale to as high as possible because *"Hey, you never know if they're going to come back! Maximize your sale now."*

I've got to start by saying if you're working with the later mentality you should close up shop. If your business isn't guaranteed to bring people back in, you should lock your doors now. *No magical amounts of one-off sales are going to make you a viable business.* The ultimate success of your business is going to be longevity, and we're not talking about sales-streaks, we're talking about your long-term customer life cycle.

In retail you try to lure customers back with coupons, mailers, weekly deals, and any other hype or gimmick your marketing team can dream up… "Studies show…research supports…The University of blah blah blah…" fills your ears almost daily. Hours upon hours of training and retraining occur each day, week, or month, all striving to increase profits but ultimately they lead to failure and rarely produce lasting results. Sometimes it seems like new metrics come up every week.

The worst thing you could ever do is to tie pay-for-performance to metrics. This will always lead to your staff *game the system* and ultimately committing fraud or manipulating their metrics. Every call center I have ever experienced does this. Ever have a call "dropped" while speaking to customer service on the phone? If I had to logically quantify the percentage of "drops" that were intentionally done by specialists who were either tired of your voice or manipulating their call metrics, I would be inclined to say that well over 90% of those cases were due directly to manipulation of a metric.

To a phone specialist, your worth is summed up in about 600 seconds. That's the typical call center metric goal for a total call time. Now you can begin to see where the metric fallacy starts to hurt your business. If they can't solve your issue within their allotted time, then they find a way to get you off of the phone, whether or not your issue has been resolved.

Rewards programs are supposedly great tools that send customer's notices or emails promoting a big sale or providing coupons to reel them back into a sale. In theory this makes sense. Add it to a metric and you're doomed for failure. All of those pamphlets that have that new customer number for joining the rewards program? All a waste of money. What's really happening? Is your store really getting 200 new customers to join your rewards program every week? Great job team? Or are the cashiers simply typing in those numbers on the brochures and blindly dropping the form into the customer's bag without informing them?

How about incentives for a retention specialist to save more customers by tying it to a bonus payout? "WOW, they are saving a LOT more customers, this must be working?" Or…are they manipulating the way they track their "saves"?

It's been said that studies show once you start measuring something, you see improvement. I'd like to toss that old rhetoric right out the window. Once you start measuring something, your staff starts trying to figure out how to manipulate reporting. *Any executive who honestly believes that metrics for customer service provide real value to customers and will help to ensure repeat business need to pull their heads out of the clouds.*

If you're going to measure one thing, or ask one question...it should be whether or not your customer is coming back. *If they aren't, you're not a successful business.*

How about an average ticket metric? Sounds good in theory. What it turns out becoming is an annoyance to your customer. Every pushy cashier that slows down their checkout time by asking for several thousand add-ons just makes the customer cringe at the thought of returning. They even rehearse their rejection statements and proactively interject and interrupt the attempt. Take the hint; this doesn't work for long-term growth. It goes back to the "hurry and sell them the entire store because they may never come back" mentality. *It simply doesn't work.*

If a customer can enter into a transaction with your company and walk away with a product or service that meets their needs and has received welcoming customer service, they will return. If you're going to waste your customer's time (and paying many extra bodies to create and extrapolate your metric data mines) you might as well ask the question that really matters.

Don't ask "how likely are you to...", "would you recommend...", or any other silly question that the bean counters swear will determine your stock valuation. Walk over to your customer at a restaurant, or ask your customer at the register, or ask your caller on the phone... "Will you be back?" or "Will you continue using our service?" or any variation that gets the same principle out. Not theoretically, not altruistically, not forced, not because you don't want to hurt my feelings... simply put, will you return or continue service with us? This is the only thing that matters. If you've so upset a customer that they aren't willing to return, wouldn't you want to know about it? Wouldn't you want to avoid it like the plague?

What if your very attempts at improving customer service by including metrics was the very same process causing your customer service breakdown?

Imagine an employee not having a manager breath down her throat about a metric, and instead, simply being able to serve and help their guest with no strings attached?

But *why* would anyone work this way? What is the motivation?

It's simple really, it's called a paycheck. No, you don't get a bonus for these metrics, you simply get to keep working here, after all we are paying you to do your job, and if you're doing your job all of the metrics will fall into place on their own. Take some of the money you're saving from removing your metric-based incentives and slightly boost your employee wages. It doesn't even have to be a 1 for 1 swap. Take your previous year's company-wide incentive payout, cut it in half and redistribute into a fixed wage. Keep employees that buy into your culture, and promote the others to customer (let them go).

It is a sincere injustice to shareholders and other stakeholders to be force fed a million different metrics in relation to how customers are interacting with your company. What the back office should really be looking at is how many customers are coming back. If most customers are returning, you're doing well by your customers. If you are bleeding out customers, your focus needs to change.

Manage that change and take back control of your business.

One last word of advice for your operation:

Leadership

The right People

Once you've established the right leadership team, you can begin to focus on your people.

There are basically three camps of people assumed in this text.

The first are the people who are willing to learn and onboard with your organization plans. They may not have the skill-set you need now but these individuals may need some training to help make them proficient but are truly willing to work with you.

The second are people that are skilled but unwilling to buy-in to your operation. They may be good at what they do, but they have a relaxed attitude and simply won't do what you've asked in your operation. They either disagree with or don't see the benefit of doing the things you've asked, and simply won't - no matter how much you train, explain, or help them to understand.

The third are those who create a negative work environment. If despite your best efforts to train, comfort, and come alongside people they continue to make your workplace uncomfortable or hostile, you need to cut these people loose. They may fit into either of the above categories but their extreme behavioral shifts or lack of respect for coworkers will not create a healthy environment for your staff or your guests.

If you invest in your people, you will see returns in your operation.

www.ingramcontent.com/pod-product-compliance
Lightning Source LLC
Chambersburg PA
CBHW070331190526
45169CB00005B/1850